W9-BZW-953

The American Mosaic
Immigration Today

Refugees

Sara Howell

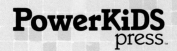

PowerKiDS press.

New York

Published in 2015 by The Rosen Publishing Group, Inc.
29 East 21st Street, New York, NY 10010

First Edition

Editors: Jennifer Way and Norman D. Graubart
Book Design: Andrew Povolny
Photo Research: Katie Stryker

Photo Credits: Cover John Moore/Getty Images News/Getty Images; pp. 4, 9 Stringer/AFP/Getty Images; p. 5 Paula Bronstein/Getty Images News/Getty Images; p. 6 Michel Setboun/Hulton Archive/Getty Images; p. 7 pablographix/iStock/Thinkstock; p. 10 Stuart Monk/Shutterstock.com; p. 11 Sixninepixels/Shutterstock.com; p. 12 Kevin Weaver/Hulton Archive/Getty Images; p. 13 David Sacks/Digital Vision/Thinkstock; p. 14 James Steidl/Shutterstock.com; p. 15 Blend Images - Hill Street Studios/Brand X Pictures/Getty Images; p. 16 Charles Taylor/Shutterstock.com; p. 17 Steve Heap/Shutterstock.com; p. 18 Mark Ralston/AFP/Getty Images; p. 19 Dbvirago/iStock/Thinkstock; p. 20 Jupiter Images/Stockbyte/Thinkstock; p. 21 George Jones III/Photo Researchers/Getty Images; p. 22 Nick White/Photodisc/Thinkstock.

Library of Congress Cataloging-in-Publication Data

Howell, Sara.
Refugees / by Sara Howell. — First Edition.
     pages cm. — (The American mosaic: immigration today)
Includes index.
ISBN 978-1-4777-6741-2 (library binding) — ISBN 978-1-4777-6742-9 (pbk.) — ISBN 978-1-4777-6649-1 (6-pack)
1. Immigrants—United States—History—Juvenile literature. 2. United States—Emigration and immigration—History—Juvenile literature. 3. Citizenship—United States—Juvenile literature. I. Title.
JV6450H697 2015
325'.210973—dc23
                                        2014002349

Manufactured in the United States of America

CPSIA Compliance Information: Batch #WS14PK1: For Further Information contact Rosen Publishing, New York, New York at 1-800-237-9932

Contents

Who Are Refugees?

Each year, many people move to the United States and other countries looking for a better life. They may move to find jobs or to be close to family. These people are called **immigrants**. There are about 40 million immigrants in the United States today.

The Haitians on this boat are being helped by the U.S. Coast Guard. When they get to America, they will be considered refugees.

These are refugees from Sudan. They are living in a country called South Sudan, but some of them will immigrate to other countries.

Some people leave their home countries for other reasons. Those who have left their home countries to find safety are called **refugees**. Each year, a little more than 70,000 refugees are given permission to live in the United States. Many come from countries such as Iran, Burma, and Bhutan.

A Dangerous Journey

The people on this boat are escaping Vietnam. Vietnamese refugees settled in the United States, Canada, Australia, and other countries.

Refugees have left their country because they fear for their safety. They often must flee their homes quickly and leave many things behind. Refugees are looking for another country or government to give them protection, or **asylum**.

In the 1970s, many people in Vietnam feared for their safety after the end of the Vietnam War. The Vietnamese government sent those who had disagreed with them to prison camps. The only way for many to escape Vietnam was by boat. More than 800,000 Vietnamese refugees were given asylum in the United States. In recent years, most refugees in America have come from Iraq, Bhutan, and Burma.

Some refugees fly to America. Occasionally, the American government will help them escape their home countries by airplane.

Seeking Asylum

People seek asylum for many reasons. They may have been **persecuted**, or attacked because of their race or beliefs, in the past. They may fear being persecuted in the future. Some people around the world are persecuted because of their political beliefs. Others are in danger because of their religion.

Not everyone seeking asylum is given permission to live in the United States. A person may be considered **inadmissible** if he has been in trouble with the law or if he has certain health problems. The US government may also deny asylum to people they believe are a danger to the United States.

These Egyptian Christians are celebrating Christmas. Christians are sometimes persecuted in Egypt, so many have sought asylum in America.

Applying for Asylum

The first step in applying for asylum is getting a **referral** to the US Refugee Admissions Program, or USRAP. People referred by the United Nations High Commissioner for Refugees or a US embassy have **priority** over other applicants. Asylum seekers with close family members in the United States are also given priority.

This is the United Nations building in New York City. The UN has helped millions of refugees find safety in other countries.

USCIS workers must do a lot of paperwork and research before granting asylum.

Once an asylum seeker is referred to USRAP, she will get help filling out an asylum application. This application can also include a person's spouse and any unmarried children who are under 21. The asylum seeker will then be interviewed by an official from US **Citizenship** and Immigration Services, or USCIS.

Coming to the United States

Once a person's application for asylum is approved, he has permission to stay in the United States. Refugees are given **loans** to help pay for their travel. They are also given medical exams and help finding doctors if they have any health problems.

Often, refugees are escaping places without good medical care. Doctors in the United States can give them advice on how to stay healthy in their new country.

Finding a place to live can be difficult in a new country. Mercy Housing is an organization that works with ORR to help find housing for refugees.

A part of the US government called the Office of Refugee Resettlement, or ORR, works closely with refugees. They help newly settled refugees learn about the United States. They help them settle in areas that have the services they will need. They also help refugees find jobs and understand any benefits available to them.

The Rights of Refugees

The Constitution contains the Bill of Rights. The Bill of Rights lists some of the most important rights that Americans have.

As soon as they arrive in the United States, refugees have many important rights. A right is something that people should be allowed to do. Refugees have many of the rights listed in the US **Constitution**. These include the right to belong to any religion they choose and the right to own property. Refugees have the right to get an education, own businesses, and choose where to live.

Like everyone in the United States, refugees are protected by all US laws. This means that no one is allowed to hurt them or steal from them just because they are refugees.

You can talk to police officers about your rights as an American refugee. Police officers know about American laws.

Working and Traveling

Refugees have the right to find jobs as soon as they arrive in the United States. Certain forms prove to employers that a refugee has permission to work. Many refugees start their own businesses and create jobs for other US workers.

PASSPORT

United States of America

You have to be a US citizen to get an American passport. This is why refugees must get a special travel document if they want to travel outside of the United States.

2012 Estimated Tax

...sury ...ce

...king a payment of estimated tax by check or money order. Mail this ...eck or money order payable to "United States Treasury." Write your ...er and "2012 Form 1040-ES" on your check or money order. Do not send ...or attach, your payment with this voucher.

Your last name

Payr

Tax and Credits

38
39a

Amou
Check
if:

Standard

Form 1040 (2011)

Form 1040

Form 1040

Department of the Treasury—Internal Revenue Service (99)
U.S. Individual Income Tax Return

2012

OMB No. 1545

For the year Jan. 1–Dec. 31, 2012, or other tax year beginning , 2012, ending , 2

Your first name and initial	Last name
If a joint return, spouse's first name and initial	Last name

Home address (number and street). If you have a P.O. box, see instructions.

City, town or post office, state, and ZIP code. If you have a foreign address, also complete spaces below (see instructions).

Foreign country name | Foreign province/county

Head of
the qual
child's

iling Sta

This is a tax return form from the US government. Like other US workers, refugees pay taxes on the money they earn.

Refugees have the right to move freely within the United States. Many move to new cities to find jobs or be closer to family members. If a refugee would like to travel to other countries, she must get a special travel document from the US government. This document allows refugees to visit other countries and return legally to the United States.

From Refugee to Resident

Sometimes the problems that led a refugee to leave his home country will be fixed and the refugee can return home. Very often, though, refugees live the rest of their lives in the countries where they resettle. In the United States, refugees must apply to become **permanent residents** after living here for one year.

These Filipino refugees are leaving a refugee camp in Tacloban, Philippines. Some will apply for asylum in America.

Sometimes, refugees start businesses that sell products from their home countries. This often helps them feel closer to home.

To become a permanent resident, a refugee must send an application to the US government. The application includes many forms and documents and two copies of a recent photograph. Each member of a family must fill out a separate application.

The Path to Citizenship

After living as a permanent resident for five years, refugees are allowed to apply for US citizenship. Citizenship comes with many rights and responsibilities. One important right that only citizens have is the right to vote in elections. Elections allow citizens to choose the people who will serve in the US government.

Applicants for citizenship must pass a citizenship test. Reading books about how the US government works can help an applicant do well on the test.

These people are taking part in a citizenship naturalization ceremony. After they promise to defend the United States, they will be new citizens!

To apply for citizenship, permanent residents must fill out an application. Their history and background will be checked. They will also be interviewed to make sure they can read, speak, and write English and that they understand how the US government works.

The American Mosaic

Refugees leave their homes looking for safety and protection. Coming to the United States gives them a chance to start new lives. Soon after arriving, most refugees become active and contributing members of their communities.

The United States is sometimes described as a **mosaic**, or a picture made by fitting many small pieces together to create a larger work. Each day, citizens, immigrants, refugees, and many others come together to create and enjoy the culture of their country!

All Americans have ancestors who came from somewhere else, so we can all relate in some way to the refugee experience!

Glossary

asylum (uh-SY-lum) Protection given by a country to persecuted people.

citizenship (SIH-tih-zen-ship) The legal right to live forever in a certain country.

Constitution (kon-stih-TOO-shun) The basic rules by which the United States is governed.

immigrants (IH-muh-grunts) People who move to a new country from another country.

inadmissible (ih-nud-MIH-suh-bel) Not able to be admitted.

loans (LOHNZ) Money given to people that must be paid back later.

mosaic (moh-ZAY-ik) A picture made by fitting together small pieces of stone, glass, or tile and pasting them in place.

permanent residents (PER-muh-nint REH-zuh-dents) People who are not citizens but who have the right to live and work in a country forever.

persecuted (PER-sih-kyoot-ed) Attacked because of one's race or beliefs.

priority (pry-AWR-uh-tee) Preferential status that allows one to get something sooner.

referral (rih-FER-ul) The official act of directing someone to the place where he or she can get help.

refugees (reh-fyoo-JEEZ) People who leave their own country to find safety.

Index

Websites

Due to the changing nature of Internet links, PowerKids Press has developed an online list of websites related to the subject of this book. This site is updated regularly. Please use this link to access the list:

www.powerkidslinks.com/mosa/refug/